MANY ARE CALLED
FEW CHOOSE

The Death-Defying Pursuit of Yahweh

WILLIAM A. ULSH, JR.

D1528776

KUDU

Many Are Called—Few Choose: The Death-Defying Pursuit of Yahweh

by William A. Ulsh, Jr.

Published by Kudu Publishing

Trade Paperback ISBN: 978-0-9849294-7-4
eBook ISBN: 978-0-9849294-8-1

Available in Amazon Kindle, Apple iBooks and Barnes & Noble Nook formats.

Scriptures taken from The World English Bible (WEB) (*www.ebible.org*).

Scriptures taken from The Message. Copyright © 1993, 1994, 1995, 1996, 2000, 2001, 2002. Used by permission of NavPress Publishing Group

Cover Design: Martijn van Tilborgh

DEDICATION

To every man who has the courage to call himself a "son of righteousness" and the integrity to conduct himself accordingly. May you be unshakably established in the Kingdom of Christ as you set the standard for everyone around you.

CONTENTS

ENDORSEMENT

The basis for this book began during a Sunday message preached in 2011. The intention was to quote the well-known passage found in Matthew 22:14: "Many are called, but few chosen" (WEB). What came out was very different: "Many are called, few choose." There was an immediate recognition within my spirit that this was a deeply profound revelation that came directly from Holy Spirit. From that moment it was my objective to discover the meaning behind this revelation. The following pages are really just the beginning of understanding this deep calling unto deep truth, and all credit must go to Holy Spirit, my Guide, my Comfort, and my Endorsement.

FOREWORD

Did you think you were gonna die?
I didn't think I was gonna die; I knew I was
gonna die.
—60 MINUTES INTERVIEW WITH DAKOTA MEYER
CONGRESSIONAL MEDAL OF HONOR RECIPIENT

I have some questions: Why is the kingdom of God not established on this earth, specifically, in this nation? How come we are not seeing the fulfillment of Christ's promise that we would do the things that He did, and even greater?

Where is the awesome display of Yahweh's power that started with the outpouring of Holy Spirit at Pentecost and should have exponentially increased since then? More troubling than those questions is this: why aren't more people asking those questions?

Here's the answer: we are a bunch of whining, sniveling cowards; the whole lot of us. There is not a man among us who has the guts or the fortitude to be the man of God that we make ourselves out to be. We flock to large sanctuaries and listen to smiling preachers who tell us everything's going to be alright. We watch their programs, buy their books and teaching tapes, give them our money. We do all this and still continue to lie, cheat, steal, fornicate, lust, hate, manipulate, envy, get drunk, get high,

9

curse, overeat, overindulge, overlook the needy, fill our minds with every kind of filth; it goes on. We reject men who would be spiritual fathers, men who would correct us and discipline us, men who would require an accounting of our lives and demand that we achieve the unachievable. Instead, we clamor for mommies behind whose skirts we can hide, and we have gotten exactly what we wanted.

Our religion is little more than a matter of convenience. We give it its just due—when it's convenient for us. Just make sure there's not too much talk (better yet, none at all) about things like going the second mile, turning the other cheek, giving our stuff up, going to the back of the line, taking up crosses, laying down our lives—enough already!

There is a huge disconnect between the Gospel of Christ and the Gospel of America. It's not for lack of trying; it's for lack of daring. We all know that there is none righteous, no not one; it's time to realize that there is also none courageous, no not one.

We in America don't have a clue what it means to give our lives for Christ. Gordon Conwell Theological Seminary, well-respected and very conservative, stated in 2006 that approximately 171,000 Christians are martyred each year*. Let that sink in for a minute. These are Christians who are dying for their faith. Not being laughed at or ignored or overlooked for a promotion. Dying. Sometimes entire families. And it is in these places that awesome things are happening for the Kingdom of God.

Do a search and see if you can find the record of when the last martyr was slain on this continent.

Immediately following this Foreword is the account of what is known as the Eight Martyrs of North America. It is important to note that this happened long before the establishment of the United States of America. The challenge is for you to read it through, thoroughly. Be prepared; it's graphic. If you get through it and find that this is just too much for you to stomach just go

* *http://www.worldchristiandatabase.org/wcd*

back to your refined religious sensibilities and your cowardice. But if this stirs something in you that you have never felt before, the challenge is to read on and find out if you have what it takes to recklessly and relentlessly pursue Yahweh.

May this Foreword become your *forward*.

Chapter I

RESOLUTE
The Eight Martyrs of North America

For me to live is Christ, and to die is gain.
—PHILIPPIANS 1:21

In June of 1625, three Jesuit priests made the arduous journey from France to North America. Their destination was a small convent located close to Quebec on the Saint Charles River. The task before them was enormous: bring the Good News of the gospel to the Native Americans.

It was a mission filled with tremendous obstacles and hardship. The conditions were often appallingly bad, and the people they came to minister to were unusually difficult to convince. The language barrier was an extremely complicated one, filled with complex nuances of meaning that would take years to fully master. On top of all of this was the fact that the different Native American nations were often at war with one another. Nonetheless, these men entered into this labor with great joy and devotion.

One of these priests was Father John de Brebeuf, a very large man whose size greatly impressed those to whom he ministered.

He endeavored to win their confidence and respect by engaging himself in all of the normal labors and struggles that these people faced on a daily basis. This was often made even more challenging because of the proliferation of superstition and sorcery that was a common factor in the culture of the Native Americans. But Brebeuf persevered and slowly began to make progress, even to the point of being practically recognized as a member of the Hurons.

Unfortunately, this progress was virtually stopped when the growing conflict between England and France led to near starvation of the colony, and the priests were forced to return to France in 1629. It was four years before Brebeuf could return to his work in the New World. This time he was accompanied by Father Anthony Daniel, a capable and enthusiastic man who showed a genuine gift for learning the Huron language.

Things improved even more with the arrival of Fathers Charles Garnier and Isaac Jogues two years later. But this was soon followed by an influenza epidemic that devastated the native population. All of the priests survived, but instead of seeing this as a validation of their position before God, the medicine men (who continuously opposed them) accused them of intentionally causing the sickness in order to steal their land. The priests maintained their faith and continued to minister both spiritually and physically to the sick and dying, until the epidemic finally subsided.

It seemed as if the worst was behind them. In spite of their constant labor and efforts, it took years before they began to find a measurable acceptance of the gospel. Just when they began to realize some success, another epidemic struck, this time small-pox. Many died, and this time the priests were expelled from every Huron village. This contagion lasted for three years, during which time the priests continued to minister at every opportunity, all the while being made more aware that even greater danger was yet to come. They could hardly have guessed what was still before them.

The mission was in desperate need of supplies, so an expedition, under the leadership of Jogues, was organized. It took a month to reach their destination. They began the difficult return trip with the supplies, as well as another priest, Rene Goupil. On the second day they were attacked by a ferocious group of Iroquois. All were captured and subjected to terrible torment.

It began with something called "running the gauntlet." The prisoners were forced to run between two lines of warriors, each of whom held large clubs or rods with thorns. The beating and punishment from this alone was enough to bring them to the brink of death. This was followed by a series of attacks that can only be defined as a display of demonic frenzy. Slashed with knives, burned with torches, gouged with fingernails, thumbs and fingers actually chewed to the bone, and, in Father Jogues' case, chewed completely off.

When the attackers tired of their torture, they stretched their victims naked on the ground, tied to stakes. But even then there was no respite; the children would throw burning embers onto their exposed bodies. Amazingly, both Jogues and Goupil survived this initial torture. But shortly afterward Jogues was forced to watch as his new-found friend was viciously struck down by a tomahawk and became the first of the Jesuits to be martyred for Christ.

Jogues remained enslaved for over a year before he was able to escape. He returned to France, but only remained there for three months before returning to the place of his calling. At first it seemed that the sacrifices Jogues had already endured had ended, for he began to enjoy a moderate success. But it was only temporary, for two years later he was beheaded, along with another young priest named John De LaLande.

Through all of this turmoil Fathers Brebeuf and Daniel continued their labor of love and sacrifice. No longer working side by side, they were in separate areas. Father Daniel was still ministering to the Hurons and had earned their respect and admiration. But there was still great animosity between the Native American nations. The village where Daniel was living was attacked, and as the inhabitants fled for their lives, he calmly walked toward the invading warriors dressed in his white robes. The attackers hesitated, then shot him down with muskets and arrows. He was scalped and partially eaten before his body was tossed into the flames of his beloved chapel.

Father Brebeuf received this news with great sadness and could only hope that he, too, was worthy of martyrdom. He soon received a new assistant, Father Gabriel Lalemant. It was not long after Lalemant's arrival that the test Brebeuf both welcomed and feared was before him. As happened with Father Daniel, the village where the priests were laboring was attacked.

They were forced to "run the gauntlet," after which Brebeuf's fingers were shredded and mangled by the frenzied warriors. He was tied to a stake with burning wood piled beneath his feet and legs. Hot coals were shoved against his neck and into his armpits. Through it all he remained silent, for he knew that if he cried out his torturers would claim victory. The enraged attackers began to cut him. Now he cried out, "Jesus, have mercy on us!" To keep him quiet burning brands were forced into his mouth. A necklace made of red-hot hatchets was placed around his neck, followed by a belt formed of bark that had been set aflame.

Brebeuf was literally being roasted, and was still able to resist crying out in pain. Instead, he offered prayer for his tormentors, one of whom responded by pouring a pot of boiling water over the priest's head. His reply: "Jesus, have mercy on us!" This infuriated his captors beyond belief. His nose was cut off by one; his lips were removed by another who also managed to chop off most of his tongue; and if that was not enough still another held a flaming torch against what remained of his mouth. One last time he cried out: "Jesus, have mercy on us!" The braves finished what they had begun by burning out his still-open eyes with a hot brand.

Father Lalemant, much smaller in stature than Brebeuf, witnessed this entire horror, and knew it was now his turn. Incredibly, even after going through the same dreadful assault, the little priest, although unconscious, remained alive. He regained consciousness sometime during the night, and immediately began to pray. He was rewarded by having his tongue cut out and his mouth filled with hot coals. But even that could not satiate the hellish hunger of his attackers. They plucked out his eyes and put more hot coals into the empty sockets. The last thing he had to endure was to have his hands cut off and the bloodied stumps seared with axe-heads made red-hot in the fire. Lalemant could take no more, and slipped into eternity as the sun rose.

The Superior of the Jesuit Order now issued an order for all remaining priests to return to the relative safety of Saint Joseph's Isle near Quebec. Father Garnier, who had long labored with Brebeuf, was now working with Father Noel Chabanel in a southern area. They received the instructions with heavy hearts and obediently, but reluctantly, made preparations to leave their mission. But neither ever made it back. Both were butchered by the very people they had come to save, their bodies tossed into the river like carrion.*

Now, take a deep breath. Don't get caught up in doctrine or theology. Simply reflect on the fact that these were devout men, brothers in the faith, believers who were willing to lay down their lives for Christ. Now think on this: Who among the men we revere today has ever come close to this kind of sacrifice? The false doctrines of the world have been seductively blended in with the gospel and, just like the world, we don't want simple ordinary men to lead us; we want celebrities.

Celebrities don't give their lives (or anything else for that matter) for anyone or anything. Celebrity is about self, and self is the opposite of sacrifice, the opposite of Christ. In our "what's in it for me?" culture, the focus is on getting what you can while you can. This fosters a spirit of watchful suspicion and chronic fear,

---

* The previous section was adapted with permission from *http://catholicism. org/eight-na-martyrs.html*

because there is always the possibility and threat of someone else stepping in and taking what we want for ourselves. This is not isolated; it is epidemic.

Example: Black Friday, November 25, 2011, the biggest retail day of the year. People literally camped out overnight on the sidewalk in front of the stores they believed had the best deals. When is the last time you went to church and found a line of people who had come the previous day and stayed overnight to get the best seats? Here are the statistics: several people are shot, at least one is stabbed, others are beaten and trampled and one person pepper-sprays a whole group of people, all because they thought someone else was going to get what they thought was rightfully theirs. This is what fear does: it makes us lash out indiscriminately, almost convulsively, like a cornered animal, just like those who so viciously tortured and killed the men remembered above.

The men remembered above. How did they do it? How did they overcome fear and unwaveringly face such horrific trials? Darkness is not the opposite of Light; it is the absence of Light. The same logic holds true with fear: fear is the absence of faith. It is fear that paralyzes and frustrates the advance of the Kingdom of God. It is fear that keeps us from speaking up and speaking out. Fear is a spirit (2 Timothy 1:7), and as a spirit fear has a certain intangible substance and essence that we usually fail to recognize. We think it's just a "thing."

We think the same thing about sin. We are wrong. Sin is not just something we do. Sin is an employer—it pays wages! (Romans 3:23). Sin is a powerful force, an entity in and of itself. We have been taught that the satan somehow controls sin. That's a lie that he has successfully passed on for centuries. The truth is that the satan has never been able to put a bridle in sin's mouth. He needs sin, but sin doesn't need him. Sin is going to do what it's going to do with or without the satan. It is your *sin* that will find you out! (Numbers 32:23). We refer to the devil as the enemy, but our real enemy is sin. What makes us think that Yahshua laid down His glory, took on the form of man, lived a perfect life, died the cruelest death, and then rose again just to give the devil a black eye? Yahweh has angels that can manage the satan!

Consider the conflict that arose between the satan and Michael the Archangel over the disposition of Moses' body. The devil is leaning over the corpse when someone taps him on the shoulder. He turns around.

The satan: "Hey Mike! Haven't seen you in a while. What's going on?"

Michael: "You tell me."

The satan: "Oh, same old same old. Just going to and fro throughout the earth, taking care of business. Just came across a dead body. You know, if I didn't know any better I'd say it was Moses! (He looks closer) My God! It IS Moses! How tragic! I mean, right over there is the promised land! To have come so far and get so close and to die now...It's just not right. Hey, tell you what I'm gonna do. I'll take his body and put it in the most amazing mausoleum ever. I know just the place. After all, he deserves it. So, if you'll just get out of my way..."

Michael: "I don't think so."

At that point it was on! Why would the devil want the body of Moses, and why would he want to honor it by putting it in the greatest monument and mausoleum ever constructed? Because he knew that men would throng to it and, ultimately, worship it.

Been to visit Moses' Mausoleum lately?

There is no mausoleum because Michael defeated the satan and hid the body of Moses. In fact, he did such a good job of hiding the body that those demons that have been given the singular assignment of finding it have never done so, and never will.

So, it goes without saying that Christ's purpose was far greater than defeating the devil: He came to destroy the power of sin. Sin, once so completely abundant, has been utterly overwhelmed and trampled by the infinitely greater power of grace. Make no mistake about it—grace is not the ephemeral, gossamer-winged and fragile thing we have been duped into thinking it is; grace is a *warrior* and it will not stop until it wins.

What does that have to do with fear?

Everything.

All sin can do is threaten us with death. Death is the source of all fear. *But Christ has conquered death!* Christ, having been raised from the dead, dies no more! Death has no dominion over Him (Romans 6:9). In Revelation 1:18, He declares: "I am He Who lives, and was dead, and behold, I am alive forevermore! Amen! And I have the keys of hell and death!"

Hallelujah! What awesome news that is! The problem is that most of us don't seem to know that yet. Or, if we do, we certainly don't live up to it.

But these men who gave their lives knew it. Somehow, these unyielding men shook off the specter of fear that has so thoroughly ensnared so many of us. They did it through faith, faith in Yahshua the living Christ. It was a faith that turned the tables on fear, a faith that defied the grip of terror that death has held over mankind for so very long. Where is that kind of faith today?

The darkest night can be penetrated by a single candle, and the light of a single candle, if used wisely, can push back the darkness completely. So it is with faith. Trusting God for what is not as if it were, choosing to believe His Promise and to put their confidence in the invisible rather than the visible, these men left fear behind and pierced the darkness around them with the glorious light of their Lord and Savior. They did the unthinkable and in so doing paved the way for the salvation of countless souls, and for themselves won eternal glory and honor. They were just men, like us.

If they could do it, we can, too.

Resolute or afraid?

Choose.

Chapter 2

REBELLIOUS
The Apostles

Remembering Civil War Sergeant Phil Hamline, one of his brothers in arms stated, "I can say without hesitation that I never knew a man who had a more absolute trust in God or one that made his religion more completely and beautifully a part of his daily life. No man in the company was more universally respected, and no one better deserved respect. Deprecating war, loving and praying for peace, he was fighting for his government as the performance of a sacred duty he owed to it and his God. He had the most implicit faith in an 'overruling Providence' and seemed to feel that—no matter what happened to him personally—all that he was fighting for was certain to be accomplished. The results were splendid vindication of his sublime faith. His memory is a sweet perfume from the days of my association with him and is a halo over the service."*

The night of Christ's betrayal was also the night of His abandonment. Boastful words of loyalty disintegrated into ash as each disciple scattered in an effort to save his own skin, leaving the Savior to face His unspeakably horrific destiny in complete solitude.

---

* James A. Wright & Steven James Keillor, *No More Gallant a Deed: A Civil War Memoir of the First Minnesota Volunteers* (Minnesota Historical Society Press: 2001), 317.

On one of the lunar missions the astronaut who remained with the module that orbited the moon was called "the loneliest man in the world" as he went around the dark side. Poignant, but not true. No One was ever more alone than Christ as He obediently followed the appointed trajectory that catapulted Him across the incomprehensible darkness that is sin.

Granted, this was a terrifying time, and it is stretching things to be too critical towards the disciples. But Yahshua had emphatically told them about this several times. But He had also told them that after His betrayal and death He would rise again! Yet the fear that arose in those men was so great that they not only deserted their Messiah, they forgot His Word, and in forgetting they missed out on actually witnessing the single greatest event of all time: the resurrection of Yahshua.

Read the Scripture again, for the first time:

> He is not here, for He has risen, just like He said!
> —MATTHEW 28:6, WEB

This was the announcement of the angel to the women who had come to the tomb. Virtually every demonstration we see today of the resurrection shows Yahshua exiting the tomb after the stone is rolled away. That is patently wrong. Christ had risen and exited the tomb long before the angel rolled the stone away. The Lamb Who was slain but Who lives forevermore walked right through that rock wall just as He would later walk right through the door to the hiding place of the disciples. This is the moment that defines all other moments, the divine hinge upon which all of eternity turns. If there was ever an event that deserved a witness this was it! Surely, someone would have remembered and ventured out to receive Him, to be there to welcome and worship Him. Imagine! Walking in the garden in the cool of the day with the Life and the Resurrection!

Christ stepped into the garden to be greeted by—no one. The angels who had heralded His birth were not there because this was not about them. This was about redemption, the redemption of mankind.

But there was no man waiting to greet the Risen Redeemer.

Imagine a soldier returning home from war. He has told his family and closest friends all the necessary details of his arrival. Joyful anticipation mounts with each passing second as the moment of reunion approaches. The plane touches down, he makes his way to the appointed place, searching for familiar faces. But no one is there. The terminal is empty. Who could blame him for catching a taxi and taking a ride around town, in no hurry to get home to the ones who were in no hurry welcome his return? Understanding this helps to explain Christ's almost cryptic treatment of the disciples in the hours immediately following the resurrection.

The sad truth is that the stone was only rolled away by the angel so that the late-arriving, disbelieving and quivering disciples could see that He was gone. Even then, they did not know what to make of it and returned to their hiding place firmly in the grip of their abject fear. Not a good start.

Less than two months later, these very men had become galvanized into the most earth-shaking group the world has ever seen. Everywhere they went they brought the electrifying news of a risen Savior Who had paid the awful price of sin. They incited and provoked and were accused of turning the world upside down for the cause of the Christ and His Kingdom. How did this happen? What could possibly have occurred that resulted in such a remarkable transformation, that men who were once completely cowed by fear were now bastions of unshakeable faith?

We are familiar with the terms BC (Before Christ) and AD (Anno Domini) which are used to determine years in the Julian and Gregorian calendars. Many Believers will refer to the time prior to their acceptance of Christ as Savior as BC. For the original disciples a far more significant application would have been BR (Before Resurrection) and AR (After Resurrection), because it is this which finally and ultimately defined their unconquerable conviction.

Christ was with His disciples for forty days after His resurrection. He spoke to them of the Kingdom, and gave them specific instructions, but, most importantly, He "…showed Himself to be alive by many infallible proofs" (Acts 1:3). The key word here is infallible. Not to be questioned. It is beyond debate.

Somewhere during those forty days they finally got it: *death had been conquered!* The single greatest fear of each of their lives (and ours as well) was destroyed, annihilated, obliterated, extinguished, eradicated, eliminated, and exterminated, once and for all. Is it possible to be any clearer than that? Christ was alive—no, not was, *is! Christ is alive!* If any one of them had had the presence of mind to remember His words and had been present to actually witness His resurrection the following forty days would have seemed almost redundant.

This immensely profound, deep calling unto deep truth and understanding, combined with the awesome empowerment of Holy Spirit (as described in Acts 2), is what mobilized these men and turned them into supremely fearless oracles for God.

Numerous times during His ministry (BR), Christ severely admonished His men for their displays of fear. Remember, these were men who spent a great deal of time together. That creates a strong bond of camaraderie that, in turn, lends itself to open and honest communication. In other words, forget about the soft and often feminine appeal that has so often characterized our idea of Yahshua. The Son of Man was a man's Man, and when He told His men to stop it He meant stop it!

> "What's the matter with you? Haven't you learned anything? Do not be afraid!"
>
> —(AUTHOR'S PARAPHRASE)

The passage where Peter is called to walk upon the water is one of the best known stories and one of the most poorly understood and interpreted. The vast majority of the present-day church believes that the message in this passage is: don't take your eyes off of Jesus.

Rubbish! That's not the message at all.

If that was the message Yahshua would have asked, "Peter, why did you take your eyes off of Me?" Instead, He reproved His man by asking, "Why were you afraid?"

It was impossible for Peter to walk upon the water. But he did it—until he started checking out the wind and the waves and, subsequently, allowed fear to enter in. Suddenly, his human reasoning took over: "Hey man! This isn't possible! You're gonna die!" Enter fear, and Peter immediately begins to sink. Fortunately, Yahshua was nearby and saved him.

Not many days later (AR) Peter encountered a man who was born without bones in his ankles and feet. There were people all over the place, lots and lots of opportunity to look like a fool. Now get this: it was as impossible for that man to stand on solid ground as it was for Peter to walk upon water. But with massive faith that forcibly pushed aside all other considerations, Peter takes this man by the hand and literally jerks him off the ground as he proclaims, "In the Name of Yahshua of Nazareth—walk!" Remember, there are people around; lots of people; that equals the enormous prospect for failure. But Peter didn't stop to wonder, "What if this doesn't work?" He just did it. And here's something else to consider: this lame man was not asking for healing. All he wanted was some loose change. But the next thing he knows he is actually lifted into the air, and somewhere between lift-off and landing, he is healed! He lands on his feet, uncertain and unsure (remember, he has never walked a day in his life), but he is standing! He's holding onto Peter's shoulders, faltering, working to find his balance, but for the first time in his life he is looking straight into the eyes of another man who is standing before him. His eyes widen in amazement. He takes one uncertain step, then another, and before long he's walking and soon he is leaping and shouting! All he wanted from Peter was some money. In terms of faith or belief or desire the lame man contributed absolutely nothing to his healing—it was entirely a manifestation of the faith demonstrated by Peter.

Without faith we cannot please God. As mentioned earlier, the opposite of faith, the enemy of faith, the undoing of faith is fear. Fear has many faces: embarrassment, failure, loss, pain, insecurity, and much more. But the foundation of all fear is death.

What was the first great lie? "You shall not surely die."

If death is conquered then fear is conquered, and when fear is conquered faith will soar without restraint or restriction. It doesn't have to be summoned or invoked. It is simply and powerfully released. Blind eyes are opened. Deaf ears hear. Withered limbs are made whole. The dead live. Demons are cast out. Addictions are wiped away. This is faith's legacy, promise, and purpose, and the only thing that stands in its way is fear.

Many of you are familiar with 2 Timothy 1:7: "We have not been given the spirit of fear but of power, love and a sound mind." But are you aware of the Word that immediately follows this verse?

> Therefore do not be ashamed of the testimony of our Lord, nor of me His prisoner, but share with me in the sufferings for the Gospel according to the power of God, Who has saved us and called us with a holy calling, not according to our works, but according to His own purpose and grace which was given to us in Christ Jesus before time began, but has now be revealed by the appearing of our Savior Jesus Christ, Who has *abolished death* and brought life and immortality to light through the Gospel...
>
> —2 TIMOTHY 2:8–10, EMPHASIS ADDED

When we get this firmly established in our minds we become unstoppable. Like Paul we will defy the source of all fear and cry out, "Death—where is your victory?"

The disciples were in rebellion—like Yahshua they rebelled against the religious system, but even more importantly, they rebelled against the ancient and unshakeable fear that had its source, its life and its power in the specter known as death.

The amazing event of the lame man was followed by even more remarkable stuff. Peter was so beyond being afraid, so filled with divine empowerment that people tried to find out his itinerary so that they could put the sick on the side of the street where his shadow would fall! Imagine what would happen if men with that kind of courage began to walk our streets today! What are you going to do when you come upon a group of people at the bus stop who are standing around a man who has dropped over dead? Will you stare at that corpse like everyone else and hide in the anonymity of the crowd, or will you push your way through, take that cold hand in yours and declare, "In the Name of Yahshua the Christ, wake up!"?

Peter, as well as the others, was not afraid anymore. They didn't care what anyone thought. That is being rebellious to our basic human nature. But the true rebellion was even greater than that; it was within them. They rebelled against the most fundamental of all fallen man's instincts: self-preservation. All of that was consumed and replaced by Yahshua, the Lamb Who was slain but Who lives—*lives*—forevermore!

The removal of fear caused their faith to soar like eagles, and the awesome faith that was subsequently released changed their lives, and the world, forever.

By the way:

> Peter was crucified upside down on an x-shaped cross, according to Church tradition, because he told his tormentors that he felt unworthy to die

the same way that Yahshua had died.

Matthew suffered martyrdom in Ethiopia, killed by a sword wound.

Mark died in Alexandria, Egypt, dragged by horses through the streets until he was dead.

Luke was hanged in Greece as a result of his tremendous preaching to the lost.

James the Just, the leader of the Church in Jerusalem and brother of Yahshua, was thrown down more than a hundred feet from the southeast pinnacle of the Temple when he refused to deny his faith in Christ. When they discovered that he survived the fall, his enemies beat James to death with a fuller's club. This was the same pinnacle where Satan had taken Yahshua during the Temptation.

James the Greater, a son of Zebedee, was a fisherman by trade when Yahshua called him to a lifetime of ministry. As a strong leader of the Church, James was ultimately beheaded at Jerusalem. The Roman soldier who guarded James watched amazed as James defended his faith at his trial. Later, the officer walked beside James to the place of execution. Overcome by conviction, he declared his new faith to the judge and knelt beside James to accept beheading as a Christian.

Bartholomew, also known as Nathanael, was a missionary to Asia. He witnessed about our Lord in present day Turkey. He was whipped to death for his preaching in Armenia.

Thomas was speared and died on one of his missionary trips to establish the Church in India.

Jude, another brother of Yahshua, was killed with arrows after refusing to deny his faith in Christ.

Matthias, the Apostle chosen to replace the traitor Judas Iscariot, was stoned and beheaded.

Barnabas, one of the group of seventy disciples, was stoned to death at Salonica.

Paul was tortured and then beheaded by the evil Emperor Nero at Rome in A.D. 67. Paul endured a lengthy imprisonment which allowed him to write his many epistles to the Churches he had formed throughout the Roman Empire.

John was boiled in a huge basin of boiling oil during a wave of persecution in Rome. However, he was miraculously delivered from death. John was then sentenced to the mines on the prison island of Patmos where he wrote his prophetic Book of Revelation. The Apostle John was later freed and returned to serve as a bishop in modern Turkey. He died an old man, the only Apostle to die peacefully. *

Christ is alive! Death has been conquered! Do not be afraid!

Rebellious or afraid?

Choose.

---

* *http://www.icnc.org/scratchpad/a133.htm*

Chapter 3

RECKLESS
First Minnesota

Did we not do all that men could do?
—FIRST MINNESOTA SOLDIER, JULY 2, 1863

It has been well said that nothing has shaped our nation more than the Civil War. For years this horrific conflict could have gone either way. That was certainly true for the battle of Gettysburg, where there were several opportunities for victory on each side: Little Round Top, Culp's Hill, Pickett's Charge. A lesser known moment in the battle took place on the evening of the second day, July 2, 1863. A critical point in the Union line was suddenly vulnerable to an Alabama brigade and, except for unspeakable bravery and self-sacrifice, the line would have been pierced, thus dividing the Union forces and, consequently, the battle would have most certainly been won by the Confederates, and our nation would be vastly different.

Following is an eye-witness account:

> (General) Hancock spurred to where we stood, calling out as he reached us, "What regiment is this?" "First Minnesota," replied Colvill. "Charge

those lines!" commanded Hancock. Every man realized in an instant what that order meant— death or wounds to us all, the sacrifice of the regiment, to gain a few minutes' time and save the position. And every man saw and accepted the necessity for the sacrifice; and in a moment, responding to Colvill's rapid orders, the regiment, in perfect line, with arms, at "right shoulder, shift," was sweeping down the slope directly upon the enemy's centre. No hesitation, no stopping to fire, though the men fell fast at every stride before the concentrated fire of the whole Confederate force, directed upon us as soon as the movement was observed. Silently, without orders, and almost from the start, "double-quick" had changed to utmost speed, for in utmost speed lay the only hope that any of us could pass through that storm of lead and strike the enemy.

Photo courtesy of Randy Chadwick (www.brotherswar.com)

"Charge!" shouted Colvill as we neared the first line, and with leveled bayonets, at full speed, we rushed upon it, fortunately, as it was slightly disordered in crossing a dry brook. The men were never made who will stand against leveled bayonets coming with such momentum and evident desperation. The first line broke in our front as we reached it, and rushed back through the second line, stopping the whole advance. We then poured in our first fire, and availing ourselves of such shelter as the low bank of the dry brook afforded, held the entire force at bay for a considerable time, and until our reserves appeared on the ridge we had left. Had the enemy rallied quickly to a countercharge, its overwhelming numbers would have crushed us in a moment, and we would have effected but a slight pause in its advance. But the ferocity of our onset seemed to paralyze them for a time, and though they poured in a terrible and continuous fire from the front and enveloping flanks, they kept at a respectful distance from our bayonets, until, before the added fire of our fresh reserves, they began to retire and we were ordered back.

Photo courtesy of Randy Chadwick (www.brotherswar.com)

What Hancock had given us to do was done thoroughly. The regiment had stopped the enemy, held back its mighty force, and saved the position, and probably that battle-field. But at what a sacrifice! Nearly every officer was dead, or lay weltering with bloody wounds--our gallant colonel and every field-officer among them. Of the two hundred and sixty-two men who made the charge, two hundred and fifteen lay upon the field, struck down by Rebel bullets; forty-seven men were still in line, and not a man was missing. The annals of war contain no parallel to this charge. In its desperate valor, complete execution, successful result, and in its sacrifice of men in proportion to the number engaged, authentic history has no record with which it can be compared.[*]

—Lieutenant William Lochren
1st Minnesota Infantry

Such valiant and intrepid men! With no thought for self, each man surges forward, many stepping into the place that only moments before was occupied by a now-fallen comrade. The sound of bullets whizzing just inches from their heads and bodies, the sound of bullets impacting with a sickening thud into others, even themselves, the sound of desperate cries of pain all cascade upon them. The sounds are only matched by the indescribable sights of earth, blood, blue, grey and black all merging into a cacophony of color and indiscernible noise. The horror is inexpressible. Somehow, beyond all human comprehension, they press on.

They have emptied their muskets. There is no time to reload, so those who remain, those who can still run, level their weapons and charge with bayonets. Full into the maelstrom they hurl themselves with seeming abandon, their faces and voices contorted into the surreal. The greater force cannot stand against such an onslaught, and in abject fear of this otherworldly assault the Confederate regiment breaks, falls back, and abandons their position.

This singular act of heroism achieved the impossible. These men, simply following orders and fulfilling their duty, saved the day; in saving the day they saved the battle; in saving the battle they saved the war; in saving the war they saved the nation.

This kind of valor is not restricted to the men of The First Minnesota. The intangible element of courage has been identified throughout the centuries and by soldiers of every nation and

---

[*] *http://www.gdg.org/Research/MOLLUS/mollus7.html*

creed. Certain values are of inestimable worth: leadership, loyalty, and risk-taking. Regardless of these characteristics and their contribution to heroism, there is one indisputable fact: things like this happen because fear of death is put on hold and ordinary men are therefore liberated to do the impossible and what under any other circumstance would be considered unthinkable.

So the question must be asked: if men could do something like this for their companions and their country, can we do any less for our blessed Savior and His eternal Kingdom? The sad fact is that few of us, if any, have ever come close to this kind of heroic sacrifice for God.

The religious system has basically created an army of eunuchs, unable to reproduce and more concerned about propriety and political correctness than taking a stand for righteousness and holiness. We are no more capable of charging headlong into the ranks of opposition than a flock of neutered rams. When Col. Colvill gave the command to attack on that fateful day he did not need to look back—he knew that every man was right behind him. Oh, to have such men today, men willing to give all for the Kingdom of Christ! God help the righteous man who finds the courage to attack the dark forces that have occupied his city. Even if he sounds the alarm and leads the assault he will almost certainly be alone. Those who should be with him will lag behind, waiting to see the inevitable carnage, and when it is all over they will use their twisted logic ("I told you so") to validate and justify their lack of action.

We have been conditioned to believe that it is our duty to find a way to placate and not stir up, to appease and not make waves, to promote "I'm OK, you're OK" and not offend. But there *has* to be offense! There is simply no way around it! The kingdom is suffering violence and it is the violent, the strong, the fearless, who take it *by force*! (See Matthew 11:12.) We are called to do everything we possibly can, and, once that is exhausted, to *stand*! (See Ephesians 6:13.)

We consider it some kind of blasphemy to live a life that is divisive, yet Christ Himself boldly declared that He came with a sword to do exactly that: divide.

Why are we afraid of that? Do the opinions of others mean so much to us that we will defer to them and not to the divine will and purpose of Almighty God? We apologize for coming off as "holier than thou" and go out of our way to avoid appearing to be "too spiritual to be any earthly good."

What a worthless bunch of soldiers we would make!

Here it is in a nutshell: Christ came to divide; He came to separate the men from the boys, the genuine from the phony, the faithful from the fearful; He came to identify who will hear the Voice of their Captain and run down a hill towards certain death without thought of danger, and who will not.

Reckless or afraid?

Choose.

Chapter 4

RESOLVED
The Philistines

Conduct yourselves like men, and fight!
—1 SAMUEL 4:9

Of all of the opponents of the people of Israel, the Philistines were the baddest. They were the personification and the embodiment of everything that Yahweh hated. So why are they being recognized in this book? Because they deserve it.

It was approximately 1100 BC. Eli was the High Priest. His two sons, Hophni and Phineas were priests, but they were wicked and worthless men who did not know Yahweh. They abused the offerings and sacrifices that were brought into the temple and they indulged in open sexual immorality. Eli reprimanded them, but they ignored him and he did not intervene.

There is much more to being a father than words.

Even when a man of God was sent to Eli and gave him a terrifying prophecy of judgment to come Eli did nothing. There is no evidence that he sought Yahweh's mercy, something that was available to all who genuinely seek Him, even one as wicked as

Ahab (see 1 Kings 21:25-29). The mercy of the Lord is inexhaustible; one has only to sincerely seek it. Eli did not.

This was followed by yet another opportunity. Yahweh gives a profound and frightening message to young Samuel, the lad who is living under Eli's care. Eli is aware of this and virtually threatens the boy if he does not reveal the entire Word that was spoken to him. Eli could clearly be tough on women (consider his confrontation with Hanna) and children. Impressive. Samuel complies, and further verifies what has already been prophetically declared: because Eli did not restrain his sons Yahweh's divine judgment, severe and irrevocable, was going to be released, and there would be no atonement for the house of Eli.

Ever.

Eli does nothing. He simply says, "It is Yahweh. Let Him do what seems good to Him."

Ill-informed men would marvel at Eli's composure. Deluded men would commend his calm. Deceived men would applaud his tranquility. It's not composure; it's complacency. It's not calm; it's cowardice. It's not tranquility; it's weakness. By doing nothing he curses every future generation of his own house to the judgment of God. That's not good. That's pathetic.

There's still a lot of that going around today.

Not long after this the Israelites and Philistines engage in battle. These are old foes, there are ancient scores to settle, and the fighting is vicious. On the first day of battle the Philistines overcome the Israelites and drive them back, killing about four thousand men in the process. The Israelites are greatly distressed. In their despair they come up with an unbeatable plan: they will bring the Ark of the Covenant, the very Presence of Yahweh, to the battlefield.

So they send word to Shiloh, where the Ark of the Covenant is kept, and Hophni and Phineas oversee the transport of the Ark to the battlefield. The entrance of this holy thing into the camp has a singular effect upon the Israelites. They shout so loud that the ground actually shakes. The Philistines hear this incredible sound, feel the earth quake, and wonder what is happening. Then it is clear: the God of the Israelites, Yahweh, the One Who brought them through the wilderness with such overwhelming displays of power, was now in the Israelite camp and He was going to fight for them.

The Philistines are doomed. There is no way they can beat Yahweh, and they know it. Nevertheless, in spite of their fear and the certainty of defeat, they do not retreat nor do they request quarter. Instead, they make a declaration, not to the Israelites but to themselves:

> Be strong and conduct yourselves like men, you
> Philistines, that you do not become servants of
> the Hebrews, as they have been to you. Conduct
> yourselves like men, and fight!
>
> —1 SAMUEL 4:9

They decide to fight, and to fight as men, and fear disappeared. Their motivation wasn't for the best reason, but it was sound, for they knew that if they were defeated by the Israelites they would be cruelly rewarded for all of the brutality they had shown over the years. Death was better than slavery.

> So the Philistines fought, they fought like men.
> Israel was defeated, and every man fled to his
> tent. There was a very great slaughter, and there
> fell of Israel thirty thousand foot soldiers.
>
> —1 SAMUEL 4:10

Thirty thousand dead; including Hophni and Phineas (exactly as prophesied to Eli by the man of God). All in the presence of the Ark of the Covenant, which was itself taken by the Philistines.

No greater disaster could have befallen Israel. Surely, Yahweh had abandoned His people. Or maybe it was the other way around. John Wesley wrote that the Ark of the Covenant and the ordinances of God "...were never designed as a refuge for impenitent sinners, but only for the comfort of those that repent." Similarly, Matthew Henry wrote: "Let none think to shelter themselves from the wrath of God, under the cloak of outward profession."

When news of this epic tragedy reached Eli he fell from his seat and broke his neck. It is a sad end. But this isn't about Eli, for he represents all that we should reject. It is about the Philistines, enemies of God who beat His army.

How is that possible? Let's review.

The Philistines were terrified, and rightly so. Yahweh's reputation for awesome power preceded Him. Yet the Philistines overcame their fear by appealing to the only thing they had going for them: their manhood, and this was enough to win. Granted, Yahweh used this as an opportunity to bring His judgment upon Israel, but there is a specific reason that the Scripture identifies the manly stand of the Philistines: it impressed the LORD and He honored it.

So this begs the question: if Yahweh will honor a genuine expression of manhood from a sworn enemy, how much more will He respect the manhood of authentic sons of righteousness? There is only one real problem with that—where are the authentic sons of righteousness?

There are lots of believers. There are not many sons.

Does that really make any difference? Yes, it makes a world of difference. John 1:12 tells us that "as many as received Him to them He gave power to become sons."

Look at it this way: men who are mere believers are simply men in whom Christ is predominant. Men who are sons are men in whom He is preeminent. Consider the following and consider it well:

> He is the image of the invisible God, the firstborn
> over all creation. For by Him all things were cre-
> ated that are in heaven and that are on earth, vis-
> ible and invisible, whether thrones or dominions
> or principalities or powers. All things were cre-

ated through Him and for Him. And He is before all things, and in Him all things consist. And He is the head of the body, the church, Who is the beginning, the firstborn from the dead, that in all things He may have the *preeminence*.

—COLOSSIANS 1:15–18 (EMPHASIS ADDED)

In "all things" He is preeminent: over time, space, and creation; in dignity, judgment, and jurisdiction; in power, purpose, dominion, and all of eternity. His Preeminence cannot be shared, it cannot be divided, and it cannot be measured. It is complete in its supremacy and there are no contenders.

Predominance versus Preeminence

There is a profound deep calling unto deep difference between predominance (the qualifying factor in believers) and preeminence (the qualifying factor in sons).

The man in whom Christ is predominant will gladly declare that Christ is number one in his life. The man in whom Christ is preeminent understands that Christ is the only One in his life.

The man in whom Christ is predominant is still subject to the spirit of religion and, therefore, control; he does what he does because that's the way it's always been done. The man in whom Christ is preeminent lives, moves, breathes, and has his being in Holy Spirit and, therefore, walks in divine order; his coming and going is like the wind, directed by supernatural purpose.

The man in whom Christ is predominant struggles every day to be like Christ, and faces every situation with the question "what would Jesus do?" The man in whom Christ is preeminent rests in the knowledge that he IS Christ on earth, and knows immediately what to do in any circumstance.

The man in whom Christ is predominant is constantly wrestling with sin. The man in whom Christ is preeminent wrestles with God (more about that later).

The man in whom Christ is predominant seeks forgiveness multiple times every day. The man in whom Christ is preeminent walks blamelessly before Yahweh and man; with clean hands and a pure heart he is able to climb Mount Yahweh and stand in His holy Presence.

The man in whom Christ is predominant is satisfied with the occasional display of righteousness. The man in whom Christ is preeminent will accept nothing less than holiness, all day, every day.

The man in whom Christ is predominant prays primarily in his understanding, and prays in the Spirit sporadically. The man in whom Christ is preeminent prays in the Spirit prays in the Spirit prays in the Spirit until he has something to say with his understanding.

The man in whom Christ is predominant brings to the Father a portion of whatever is left over, because "God understands." The man in whom Christ is preeminent never comes into the Presence of Yahweh without bringing his very first and best, because Yahweh is worthy.

The man in whom Christ is predominant fears the unknown. The man in whom Christ is preeminent fears only Yahweh.

The man in whom Christ is predominant quails before the storm, calling out to God to "make it go away!" The man in whom Christ is preeminent stands firmly on the Rock of his

Confidence, and with the authority, anointing, and approval of Holy Spirit speaks to the storm: "Peace! Be still!"

The man in whom Christ is predominant worries that his sin will be exposed. The man in whom Christ is preeminent can boldly proclaim that the ruler of this world has nothing in him.

The man in whom Christ is predominant is content with "just making it to Heaven." The man in whom Christ is preeminent is determined to be nothing less than an overcomer, and will be rewarded accordingly, for that which is pure will not be burned, but will be proven.

The man in whom Christ is predominant longs for the good old days. The man in whom Christ is preeminent desires to go where no one has ever gone before.

The Philistines did not know anything about any of this. In this regard they were completely clueless and clearly unbelievers. But in the absence of a preeminent trust in Yahweh, the Philistines relied on the one truly greatest thing at their disposal: their manhood—and for Yahweh that was enough.

Imagine the favor that Almighty God would pour out upon genuine men who are also legitimate sons. Just envisage the empowerment that is to be received by those for whom and in whom Christ is preeminent and who, therefore, will not be moved by any conflict. Try to picture the awesome holy sanction reserved for those who are not fearful, because they have determined, in the face of all that is terrifying, to put their confidence in a Risen Redeemer, and to conduct themselves like men.

Resolved or afraid?

Choose.

Chapter 5

RELENTLESS
Jacob

I will not let you go.
—GENESIS 32:26

Jacob was a mama's boy. While brother Esau was out exploring and hunting and doing all kinds of man stuff, Jacob stayed at home and learned to cook and sew. But as Jacob remained among the tents he also learned the value of the blessing of Yahweh, and he wanted the promise that he heard about, the divine pledge that had first been given to his grandfather Abraham and then to his father Isaac. He didn't just want it—he was consumed by it. In the spirit of 1 Corinthians 12:31 he "coveted earnestly the best...."

Esau gave little thought to these things. He reveled in the hunt, the excitement of the moment. He was the very definition of "Let us eat and drink for tomorrow we die!" (1 Cor. 15:32). It is not unfair to say that the model of the self-made man that is so respected in our society is deeply rooted in this thinking. We celebrate and indeed attempt to emulate the image of the maverick, the lone ranger, the "Marlborough" man: tough, iconic, and vague.

There's only one problem with that—it doesn't work.

These things add absolutely nothing to our culture and, most importantly, these things have no place in the Kingdom of Christ. "My way" doesn't fly with Yahweh.

Even tough guys can be brought to their knees by hunger, and that's exactly what happened to Esau. A long day of unsuccessful hunting found him begging for some of the gourmet soup for which Jacob was by that time so well-known. Mild-mannered courtesy would have dictated that Jacob simply ladle up some soup for his famished brother who claimed to be on the verge of death. But Jacob was a hunter in his own right, even better at it than Esau. He had remained in his place, the place where his targeted game was most likely to appear, and when it finally happened he seized the opportunity and took his very best shot. This wasn't just a pot of beans—it was a dainty that exuded an irresistible aroma. Esau was most likely not at the point of death (tough guys are not beyond exaggeration), but he was faint with hunger, and he walked into the snare as sure as any rabbit lured by the carrot.

Jacob sees his brother approaching. The great hunter is not exulting as usual. There is no carcass draped across his broad hairy shoulders. He is clearly exhausted with a look of near-desperation on his face.

It is time.

This is the moment that Jacob has been waiting for. He stirs the pot, releasing the enticing fragrance into the air. Then he removes fresh loaves of bread from the oven, thus causing that life-giving scent to rise and blend with the other.

Overwhelming.

In all of this Jacob has done no wrong. He proves himself wise as a serpent, harmless as a dove.

"Hey, I'm dying here. Give me some of that soup."

Without so much as a word Jacob pours a man-sized portion into a bowl and places a whole loaf of bread next to it. This treasure he holds up before Esau, and then he releases his arrow.

"Sell me your birthright."

Such impudence! Such impertinence!

Matthew Henry said that the birthright "...was Esau's by providence but Jacob's by promise. It was a spiritual privilege, including the excellency of dignity, and the excellency of power, as well as the double portion."* So this is an extraordinary thing, reserved for a select few—the firstborn son.

It is quite possible that this was not the first time that Jacob brought up the subject of the birthright. It is very obvious that it was at the forefront of his thought. It is also possible that Esau had in the past verbalized his lack of need for any such back-up. He was a man's man and could take care of himself, with or without the birthright. In any case, Esau does not seem to be overly surprised by Jacob's offer. It's important to see that Jacob does not ask for the birthright to be given or even exchanged. It is transferable, and yet he wants this transaction to be irreversible. First, he says "Sell me your birthright." Second, he says "Swear to me -right now." He made this as sure as any business contract.

What a stupid thing for Esau to do! Overcome by his appetite, he takes his place among those who follow the path that leads out of Eden; and as is always the case, he lived to regret it. How many have convinced themselves that they just can't live without that car, that house, that job, that woman, that position, that toy? So they sell out to get what they think they cannot live without, and find that, in the end, it was all just smoke and mirrors.

But Esau's action was more than foolishness: it was a profanity, a virtual slap in the face of God. He ate, he drank, he wiped his mouth on his sleeve, released a satisfied belch, and walked away.

No remorse. No regret. No birthright.

---

* *http://www.biblestudytools.com/commentaries/matthew-henry-complete/*

It doesn't end there. The day arrives when Isaac realizes that he is about to die. He calls upon Esau to provide him with a last meal before he gives his son his all-important blessing. It is a matter of debate as to whether or not Isaac is aware of the birthright transaction that has already occurred between his sons. Rebekah learns of Isaac's plan and sets into motion a plan of her own. As a result of outright and outrageous deception Isaac ends up giving his blessing to Jacob, believing that he is Esau. Esau is furious and vows to kill Jacob as soon as Isaac is dead.

Rebekah is alerted to this and sends Jacob off to live with her brother Laban for "a few days."

That "few days" turned into about forty years.

Jacob's departure is hasty—he literally leaves with little more than the clothes on his back and a staff. As he makes his way to Laban, Jacob makes a covenant with Yahweh. He declares that if God will help him and bless him that he will give Yahweh a tithe of all that he receives.

Jacob finds his match in Laban. His uncle is a crafty and cunning man. It starts with the deception of exchanging Leah for Rachael, and that truly is only the beginning. Over the years Laban unfairly changes Jacob's wages 10 times. Yet, through it all, Jacob keeps his covenant with Yahweh.

The day comes when Jacob knows he must return home. He informs Laban and seeks to settle his account and receive his just compensation. It is agreed that Jacob will take all of the speckled and streaked and spotted sheep and goats as his payment for all his years of labor. But Laban knows that Jacob is the reason that Yahweh has blessed him, and he has no intentions of letting his golden boy leave. As soon as the agreement is struck Laban surreptitiously sends all the speckled and streaked and spotted animals to fields far away, under the supervision of his own worthless sons.

Cheated again.

But Jacob receives divine revelation, and does something that seems completely preposterous. He takes sticks of green poplar, almond, and chestnut trees and strips the bark from them, causing them to be speckled, streaked and spotted. Then he puts these sticks on display at the watering troughs where the flocks came to drink.

> So the flocks conceived before the rods, and the flocks brought forth streaked, speckled, and spotted. Then Jacob separated the lambs, and made the flocks face toward the streaked and all the brown in the flock of Laban; but he put his own flocks by themselves and did not put them with Laban's flock. And it came to pass, whenever the stronger livestock conceived, that Jacob placed the rods before the eyes of the livestock in the gutters, that they might conceive among the rods. But when the flocks were feeble, he did not put them in; so the feebler were Laban's and the stronger Jacob's. Thus the man became exceedingly prosperous, and had large flocks, female and male servants, and camels and donkeys.
>
> —GENESIS 30:39–43

There was nothing magic about those sticks. The empowerment was realized in Jacob's faith in what God had revealed to him. By following that divine direction, Jacob virtually dispossessed Laban.

It is time to return, because all that blessing meant nothing in a land that was not his. Jacob gathers up all his wives and children and possessions, and manages to leave without Laban's knowledge. Of course, Laban does discover this in due time and gives chase. But his anger is tempered by divine intervention in the form of a dream, and after entering into a covenant of peace Laban returns home.

But Esau is waiting.

49

Jacob is only a short distance from home. He has already received word that Esau is coming to intercept him with four hundred men. Jacob fears the worst and comes up with the best plan he can conceive at the time: he sends his wives and children and all that he has gained ahead of him, and he finds himself in exactly the same position he was in when he first left home: alone.

He stares at the fire, running all the possible scenarios through his head. His memory of Esau's incredible anger consumes his thoughts, and every outcome in his mind is bad. How did it come to this? Is there no way out? He had been through so much over the years, and in spite of the hardships he had managed to do very well for himself. Was it all for nothing? Is this how it was going to end?

Suddenly, he is aware that he is being watched. Slowly he raises his head. There, at the very edge of the firelight, a Man is standing. A visible thrill of fear runs through Jacob like a red-hot blade. The Man is cloaked from head to toe. His Face is not visible. Even in the darkness, even through His garments, Jacob can sense that He is extremely well-built and powerful. Is it Esau? Has He come to settle the score? Jacob wants to speak, but his fear is so complete that he is incapable of speech. He slowly rises, gripping his staff in his right hand, clenching his left fist, hoping but failing to appear formidable, never taking his eyes off of the Man. They stand like this for a long moment, neither speaking, neither moving. Finally, the Man slowly raises His arms, revealing that He has no staff or anything else that can be used as a weapon. Jacob understands, and suddenly allows his staff to clatter to the ground. It is the only sound and it shatters the silence. Whatever happens here is going to be hand to hand.

The Man makes the first move, moving slowly to His left. Jacob follows suit, moving slowly to his left. The Man draws slightly closer. His face is still not visible, for it is hidden in the shadow of the cloak wrapped around His head. Nevertheless, Jacob now realizes that his opponent is not Esau. His mind is reeling; his thoughts are screaming, "Who are You? Why are You doing this? What do You want from me?" But no words escape his lips, only tortured breathing.

The space between them is growing smaller. In the growing light of the fire the Man seems to be growing Himself. Suddenly, somehow, they are no longer separated by the fire. Jacob desperately tries to recall the wrestling matches he witnessed between his father and brother when he was younger. Unexpectedly, he remembers the sting of Esau's scorn as he fled to the safety of his mother's side, unwilling to engage either father or brother in contest. But now that shame creates a new sensation within him: determination. It is none too soon, for before he even realizes what is happening the Man seizes both of his wrists, throws his right arm up, slips behind him and slams him onto the ground with a resounding thud. A loud grunt escapes Jacob as the air is virtually knocked out of him. For a moment he lies stunned, and then his new-found resolve kicks in. He pushes back against the Man and in the same movement rises to his knees. Now holding onto the Man's right arm with his own he rolls sharply, taking the Man with him. For a brief instant Jacob is on top, but the Man rolls through and disengages. They both scramble to their feet. Jacob sees what looks like a grin on the Man's Face. It looks like the Face of One Who is glad for the challenge.

Jacob does not smile back.

The conflict continues. The advantage changes constantly, with neither one able to finish with a full press. At first Jacob thinks that the Man is just playing with him. But as the night wears on he is beginning to believe that he is really holding his own and his confidence grows. The fire dies down, but the shining moon and the brilliant stars seem to provide more than enough light as they bear witness to this monumental clash of man vs. Man.

Hours pass. Sunrise is approaching. Jacob holds the advantage, pinning the Man in a scissors grip with his legs. Seeing that He is being held fast the Man does something supernatural—He touches Jacob's hip and his socket is suddenly and painfully out of joint.

Clearly, this is no ordinary Man.

If he did not know it before Jacob knows it now: he is in a contest with God Himself. Common sense demands that he let go. But with a tenacity that exceeds that of common men and common sense Jacob holds on.

The Man speaks: "Let Me go; day is breaking."

Now it really is time to release his hold. Jacob has held his ground and has nothing of which to be ashamed. And it is God speaking to him. But he will not let go, and he makes a declaration that will now define not only his own life but will set the course for all of his progeny.

"I will not let You go until You bless me!"

Such recklessness! Such relentlessness! Jacob has just surpassed sheer impertinence. He has just exceeded mere impudence.

To put it into the vernacular, Jacob has just "grown some."

But what blessing could Jacob desire? Divine protection from Esau? Some kind of supernatural intervention? Or was he so singular in his pursuit of Yahweh's blessing that this was simply the natural thing for him to ask? Regardless of the reason, the Man responds with a question. Not "What blessing would you ask of Me?" but this:

"What is your name?"

What a strange question. What does it mean? Does the Man not know Jacob's name? Of course He does! The Man wants Jacob to speak his own name so that he will confront his own character: deceiver, supplanter, swindler.

It's nothing to be proud of, but this is not the time for excuses or explanations. Jacob is dirty, exhausted, bruised, and now in great pain. It is time for simple and unadulterated truth. Of all the hardship that this night has presented to him, this is the most difficult to face. All of the years, all of the stuff, all of the deceiving, finally catches up with Jacob and he weeps uncontrollably. His chest heaves with wracking sobs as he finally collides with who he really is. Long moments pass, and then he whispers hoarsely:

"Jacob!"

Few things will set a man free faster than acknowledging and accepting who he really is. Not the edited perception that he has made for himself, but the genuine and authentic, the dirty, gritty, no-holds-barred truth. The Man, clothed in Truth, recognized this immediately in Jacob and announced the best blessing Jacob could ever hope to receive:

"You're not a liar anymore. You are a princely contender with God. Your name is Israel."

More tears flow.

Jacob doesn't let go of the Man—*Israel* does!

In adoration and gratitude that can only come from being broken by none other than the Hand of the LORD, Israel lies face down in the dirt and dust and worships. In a momentary flashback to his humanity he asks the Man His Name, to which He responds: "You know Who I Am."

Then, as quickly as He appeared, He is gone.

As was his custom, Israel names this place. To his credit he does not call it the place where he wrestled with God and won. He calls it the place where he encountered God, face to face, and his life was preserved.

The wives and children had spent a restless night. From time to time there had been strange sounds coming from the direction of the camp of the man they knew as Jacob. They could only wonder at what was happening. But as the sun rose they saw a man they did not know coming towards them. And even though he was limping he had about him an air of authority, a presence of power and purpose, and the appearance and manner of a prince.

Relentless or afraid?

Choose.

Chapter 6

REVOLUTIONARY
Paul

I bear in my body the marks of Christ.
—GALATIANS 6:17

No one will dispute the contribution of the apostle Paul, but few people truly understand and appreciate the incredible extent of his suffering for his faith and his Savior. When Yahshua appeared to Ananias in Damascus and gave him instructions regarding Saul, He concluded by saying that He was going to show what great things Saul was going to suffer for His sake. Yahshua wasn't kidding around when He said this. The list of Paul's foreboding persecutions is found in Corinthians. It is not for the faint of heart.

Paul was scourged five times. This is the same torturous cruelty that Yahshua endured just before His crucifixion. Scourging was brutal beyond measure, and was properly referred to as "the little death." To go through this horror five times is difficult to fathom. Oddly enough, there was a certain etiquette, a code of behavior, that accompanied the scourge. The maximum amount of stripes allowed under Jewish law was thirty-nine (forty less one). This was to ensure that no one ever received a number of strokes that exceeded the established limit of forty. Five different occasions of this cruel punishment added up to 195 lashes, and each lash consisted of multiple thongs which were weighted with small objects of torture which tore at the body with each blow. The resulting agony is unimaginable. It is highly unlikely that there is any man living today who has endured such malice. Truly it was spoken that he had suffered "stripes above measure." The resulting scar tissue alone had to be virtually debilitating, creating a physical condition that forced Paul to live with continuous pain.

If that wasn't enough, Paul was beaten with rods three times. Unlike scourging, there was no protocol for this punishment. One can only assume that those who were doling out this sentence did so until they were unable to continue. The effect would have been incredibly terrible. Every exposed part of the body was vulnerable to debilitating repercussions. This would have undoubtedly caused concussions and contusions, especially aggravating the already susceptible areas covered with scar tissue.

Paul was constantly being thrown into prison for his preaching and teaching. This was no small thing. Prison time during this period was a terrifying prospect for anyone. A common method of internment is found in Acts when Paul and Silas were jailed at Philippi. They were seated on the ground, most likely in horribly filthy conditions, with their feet secured by stocks. On this occasion each had already been dreadfully beaten. There was no treatment available for their wounds, no attending physician to make sure that they were being properly cared for.

At Lystra, Paul was dragged out of the city limits and was stoned. It is clear that he actually died because of this appalling action. Some believe that this may in fact be the instance to which he refers in 2 Corinthians 12:2 when he speaks of "a man I know" who had gone up into the third heaven. In any case, whatever he may have experienced at that time, a group of believers gathered around his broken body and prayed, and Paul suddenly revived, arose, and went back into the city! (Acts 14:19).

Paul was shipwrecked three times, and spent an entire night and day in the sea. This may not seem to be persecution in the sense of scourging and imprisonment, but this happened in the pursuit of his obedience to his Savior. There are few things more stressful and fearsome than being completely at the mercy of the sea.

All in all, the physical toll is almost incalculable. It is certain that Paul was not a man of great bodily stature to begin with, but whatever the case may be, he was unquestionably horribly scarred, most likely disfigured, as a result of the tortures he endured for his Savior.

It is one thing to suffer for Christ, but this certainly seems to be excessive. Why was Paul subjected to such horrific treatment?

Saul stood by while Stephen, the first martyr for Christ, was stoned to death. Saul was assenting to his death, but there is no indication that he himself threw any stones at Stephen. So why the mad and feverish assault on Believers after the fact? Maybe it was the casual but calculated remarks that followed Stephen's death. Imagine that at every gathering of the Pharisees there is some snide comment: "Saul, would you watch my coat for me? I have to go and defend the faith." Each time this kind of thing happens Saul is infuriated, until he finally reaches the point of no return. He must prove himself, and he must do it with a zeal and fervor that will put all detractors to shame forever. They gathered together in one great mob to kill one man. So brave! But now one man will bring down the entire rebellious community of Christians, and his peers can stand off to the side and hold *his* coat.

Saul utterly terrorized the Christian community. There was absolutely no mercy. He was driven by a fury that exceeds understanding. A. T. Robertson says that "...threatening and slaughter had come to be the very breath that Saul breathed, like a warhorse who sniffed the odor of battle. He breathed on the remaining disciples the murder that he had already breathed in from the death of the others. He exhaled what he inhaled. Jacob had said that 'Benjamin shall ravin as a wolf' (Genesis 49:27)."* Robertson then quotes from William Furneaux: "This greatest son of Benjamin was fulfilling this prophecy."** Robertson then continues, "The taste of blood in the death of Stephen was pleasing to young Saul (Genesis 8:1) and now he reveled in the slaughter of the saints both men and women."***

He reveled in it. An uncontrollable bloodlust had come upon him, and he drank the venom of his own hatred until he became totally intoxicated with it. Fear went before him like the noisome and poisonous mist of plague. The truly frightening part of this whole thing is that Saul actually believed he was fulfilling the will of God.

It was in this demonic state of mind that Saul approached Damascus, carrying papers that authorized him to continue his terrorization of innocent men, women, and children. His heart was as cold and hard as granite, and nothing was going to prevent him from accomplishing his evil purpose.

But nothing is always preempted by Something.

Suddenly, there was a blinding light, more brilliant than anything Saul had ever imagined. As soul-shaking as this radiance was, it was the accompanying Voice that truly shattered Saul's arrogant confidence. This Voice shook the very landscape, both of the physical realm and Saul's corrupt inner man.

"Saul! Saul! Why are you persecuting Me?"

Saul was thrown from his horse by the mere power of the Voice. He groveled in the dirt, dazed, astonished, trembling uncontrollably. Like Jacob, he asks his Assailant:

"Who are You?"

Unlike Jacob, who had already had several divine encounters, Saul truly did not know Who was speaking to him. In all of his

---

* A.T. Robertson, *Word Pictures in the New Testament* (Acts 9:1).
** William Furneaux, *The Acts of the Apostles: A Commentary for English Readers* (Oxford: Clarendon Press, 1912).
*** A.T. Robertson, *Word Pictures in the New Testament* (Acts 9:1).

vicious attacks it never occurred to him that the Yahshua Whom his victims loved and served was actually a living Savior. As such, Yahshua identifies Himself.

"I am Yahshua, the One you are persecuting."

Saul's mind lurched with this revelation. His spirit reeled as he tried to come to grips with what was happening. Yahshua? Can this be possible? Yet, the power of this divine Presence was so overwhelmingly real that Saul did not question the Voice's identity another time. Instead, he makes a much more relevant inquiry:

"Lord, what do You want me to do?"

There it is, the very essence of change and realignment. Saul calls Yahshua Lord. There is a clear and immediate recognition of true authority and dominion. Such is the power of the unveiled Christ! Beware the man who claims to have had such a divine encounter and yet remains unscathed! It cannot be done! If anyone could have withstood the onslaught of the Holy Presence of the risen Christ it was Saul. But the ravenous wolf was immediately and thoroughly subdued. In this single moment Saul was confronted with the indisputable fact that he had been terribly, terribly wrong. To his credit, he was man enough to confront his error. It is not unreasonable to conclude that he anticipated a long diatribe of correction and judgment, maybe death. After all, he had single-handedly driven the Believers of the entire region into complete despair; persecuting, imprisoning, killing. He deserved to die. But that didn't happen. Instead, he receives simple instructions.

"Get up. Go into the city. There you will be told what you must do."

Why didn't Yahshua lay it all out right then and there? For one thing, God is not in a hurry; never is. But on a much more practical level He wasn't trying to kill Saul, and he had just about had enough for one day.

So Saul rises to his feet. He is blind. The great persecutor of the saints is now led into the city by the hand. The papers are left behind, trampled into the dust, tossed about by the wind, and the chief offender is now on his way to become the chief officer, although he knows nothing about that now. Now, he is nothing more than a blind man who encountered the Holy One of Israel and was allowed to live.

Sound familiar?

Saul knows there is more that he will be told; Yahshua said so. Even though he had never heard that Voice before, he knew instinctively that every word the Voice spoke was truth and power. But he waits for three nights and three days—sightless, sleepless, not eating, not drinking. Only thinking. And awestruck.

God is not in a hurry.

In the city a righteous man named Ananias is directed by Yahshua in a vision to go to Saul and pray for him. Ananias protests: "Master, you can't be serious. Everybody's talking about this man and the terrible things he's been doing, his reign of terror against your people in Jerusalem! And now he's shown up here with papers from the Chief Priest that give him license to do the same to us" (Acts 9:13-14, The Message).

What is it that gives us the idea that it's OK to question God? Job thought he had the right to question God, too, until Yahweh set him straight:

> Then Yahweh answered Job out of the whirlwind, "Now brace yourself like a man; I will question you, and you will answer Me. Will you even annul My judgment? Will you condemn Me, that you may be justified?"
>
> —Job 40:6–8

We would do well to learn from these examples, but we continue to think it is our prerogative to question Yahweh.

Live and learn.

Ananias learned that the only recourse he had was to obey God. He found Saul and prayed for him as instructed. Something like scales fell from Saul's eyes and he could see. He rose, was baptized, ate and immediately began to enjoy the fellowship of the saints. He also started to do something else right away: He preached Christ in the synagogues, that He is the Son of God.

> Then all who heard were amazed, and said, "Is this not he who destroyed those who called on this Name in Jerusalem, and has come here for that purpose, so that he might bring them bound to the chief priests?" But Saul increased all the more in strength, and confounded the Jews who dwelt in Damascus, proving that this Yahshua is the Christ.
>
> —ACTS 9:21–22

The effect was likewise immediate, and deadly. This unforeseen turn of events absolutely infuriated the Jews who quickly plotted to kill him. He had to escape Damascus by being lowered over the wall in a basket. Thus began Paul's life and death struggle to fulfill God's will for his life.

There is a direct relationship between Paul's trials and persecutions and his unquestionable authority and persuasion. It was his revolutionary and fearless tenacity that carried him through physical and emotional persecution that would have most of us crying like little girls. It was this startling doggedness that resulted in his amazing and immense influence with God and with men, an influence that continues today. Thank God for the life and testimony of Paul!

Unfortunately, what we really need today is to exert our own influence, our own testimony. Contemporary men are looking for someone they can believe in NOW. But our ability to do this is extremely limited because we choose to remain in stealth mode, below the radar. Why do we do this?

Because it's safe.

Taking a stand in today's world usually means taking a fall, and we just aren't interested in losing whatever it is we have worked so hard to attain and, most importantly, obtain. We are focused on earthly things, temporal things, stuff that just isn't going to last.

Men are really stupid. When are we going to learn that it is the invisible that is eternal? The things we cannot see, the stuff we cannot measure, the substance we cannot weigh in a scale is the core of all that will last forever.

Every so often someone actually gets it. In January, 1956, five missionaries gave their lives for Christ while ministering in Ecuador. They were killed with spears by the very ones they had come to save. One of them, Jim Elliott, kept a journal and had entered these words a little more than six years earlier: "He is no fool who gives what he cannot keep to gain that which he cannot lose."*

Paul couldn't have said it any better.

Revolutionary or afraid?

Choose.

---

* Elisabeth Elliot, *In The Shadow of the Almighty* (Harper and Row, 1958).

Chapter 7

RADICAL
Yahshua

Not My will—Yours!

— LUKE 22:42

Society has no compunction about telling us what it takes to be men. Society is stupid. There have been many contenders and a whole lot more wannabe's, but throughout all of history there has only been one Man Who has been the full and true measure of manhood: Yahshua the Christ.

Ignorant men will say that Yahshua was born with a great advantage. The truth is that He was "…tempted in all ways as we are, yet without sin." He was a man in every sense of the word. As such, Yahshua provides for us the greatest example of living that has ever graced this earth, and it is a pattern that contradicts virtually everything that our society defines as manhood. For example, we detest the very idea of someone putting their words into our mouths. Yet this is a foundational characteristic of Christ, as He declared that He was not speaking His own words or pursuing His own agenda. Everything that came out of His mouth and everything that He did was the will of the Father.

This is critical, not only for our understanding of Yahshua the Man, but also Yahshua the Christ.

If a poll could be taken today (in this country) of all Believers there would be unanimous agreement that the best possible solution to all of our problems would be for Christ to physically appear. Oh, if only Jesus would show up! He would straighten out this mess!

Actually, that's the last thing we would want, because He would tell us exactly like it is, and there's not one of us who would like it.

Everywhere Yahshua went He caused controversy. That means He was controversial! Just about everything He ever said provoked somebody. That means He was provocative! There were times when huge crowds got really agitated with Him. That means He was an agitator!

On one occasion several thousand people had gathered to hear Christ preach. But they weren't really there for Him, and He knew it. This was like dinner theatre for them; they could see a show and get something to eat. All Christ had to do was keep healing the sick and breaking bread and these people were there to stay. But instead of catering to them, instead of pandering to their appetites, instead of assuring that He would have the biggest following possible, He said this:

> You're not here for Me. You are here because you know you will get something to eat. But I am telling you the truth when I say unless you eat My flesh and drink My blood you cannot be part of this, or of Me.

This was reprehensible. No one had ever heard anything like this before. Everyone was so offended, so disgusted, that they left. The crowd went from about ten thousand men, women, and children, to just twelve men in a matter of minutes.

Note to church growth seminar promoters: don't ask Yahshua to be your guest speaker.

For the Son it was all about obedience to the will of the Father, and the ultimate act of conformity was His death, for He was "... obedient unto death, even the death of the cross."

Yet, even before death, there was an agony that is supreme and absolute. It happened in a garden, a venue that is altogether fitting. It was in a garden that the decision, the choice, to indulge in a simple act would literally change the DNA of mankind and thrust us into darkness and death. Yahweh lost His garden and He lost His son, and He wanted them back. Everything God ever planned for His creation He planned with man in mind, and His plan to redeem the planet and its inhabitants was no different. Adam's failure did not cause Yahweh to go back to the drawing board and come up with a different plan. He always knew that a man could do it and He set out to prove it by giving us His only begotten Son. All things considered, even before Golgotha, this was put to the test in the Garden of Gethsemane.

Yahshua and His disciples had just finished what we now call the Last Supper. Judas Iscariot is not among them; he is striking a deal with the Pharisees to betray Christ. When they arrive at the Garden Yahshua moves ahead a short distance to pray. He is in unbelievable torment. He knows what is before Him, and He prays that He will somehow be delivered from the unspeakable anguish of being separated from His Father. He prays with such intensity that He actually sweats blood. Don't just read that—ponder it, meditate upon it. He sweats blood. Think about the most intense physical thing that you have ever done. Try to remember how it felt, how you thought your heart was going to burst out of your chest, how your lungs went into overdrive and screamed for more air, how every muscle in your body ached with the exertion, and how blindingly exhausted you became. Now multiply that by many times and perhaps we can gain a sense of the physical distress and emotional grief that Christ was experiencing.

Up until now, every word out of His mouth has been what He had received from the Father. But on this night, it is His own words being ripped from the fabric of His very being with excruciating turmoil.

> Father, if there is any other way, please release Me from this! Nevertheless, it is not My will but Yours that I desire.

This happens three times. This alone is an indicator of the horror to come because Christ clearly receives no answer. Father is silent. This has never happened before, not in all of eternity.

For the very first time, the Son is on His own.

Perhaps that does not seem like such a horrendous thing. But think about it: the Father, the Son and the Spirit are One. They always have been. This divine silence portends something that heretofore was not only unthinkable but also impossible: that the Father would turn away from the Son. On a human level this might seem like an almost common occurrence. But this unfathomable event compromises even the very fabric of the cosmos. Add to this the unspeakable dread of taking on the sin of the entire world and the result is a dreadfulness that eludes our ability to define or comprehend.

The sin of the entire world.

Who can conceive of it? What can we possibly refer to in this natural world that could give even the most remote understanding of what this truly meant for Yahshua? He was, after all, completely and absolutely pure before God, the only One in the entire history of mankind Who remained free from sin's terrible stain. So, in that sense, He did not deserve this. He has proven that a Man can do it! He alone could claim exemption from sin's demands. So why didn't He do that?

One word: *obedience.*

And what is the one thing, indeed, the *only* thing, that enables obedience and makes it possible?

Choice.

Yahshua chose to be obedient to the Father. THIS is what makes Him worthy of all our praise and adoration! Because if you choose to be obedient that means you can also choose to be disobedient. Anywhere along the way Christ could have thrown in the towel, and there were plenty of chances.

Following the trial in the Garden of Gethsemane, Yahshua was forcibly escorted to Caiaphas the High Priest. There He is accused by many false witnesses. But the testimony is conflicting and, therefore, of no value. Nonetheless, imagine the ignominy of being completely innocent and yet being charged by such worthless scoundrels. This took time, a lot of time with a lot of opportunity to say, "Enough!" Yet He remains silent. Finally, the high priest, seething with hypocrisy and self-righteousness, demanded: "I put You under oath by the living God: Tell us if You are the Christ, the Son of God!"

All He has to do now is maintain His silence. But this is a question He cannot ignore.

"It is as you said. Nevertheless, I say to you, hereafter you will see the Son of Man sitting at the right hand of the Power, and coming on the clouds of heaven."

This ignited a firestorm of fury. Caiaphas tears his priestly robes in his astonishment at this declaration, crying out, "Blasphemy!" There was no further need of witnesses; they had heard all they needed to hear for themselves. The wrath of Caiaphas was infectious and in moments the place erupted in hysteria. Like howling animals, they swirled around Christ, spitting, hitting, slapping, taunting Him. This goes on all night long. Remember, He is already terribly exhausted from His struggle in the Garden.

He chooses to stand, and takes it.

Obedience.

Now He is bound by these same snakes and sons of the satan. He is dragged before the governor, Pilate. Here He endures further questioning before being turned over to the soldiers for scourging.

The "Little Death." There is no way to fully understand the revulsion of this torturous persecution. The ripping and tearing of His exposed flesh defies our ability to comprehend. For the briefest of moments muscle and bone is revealed, until the gaping lacerations fill with the crimson tide of His flowing blood. The gasps of pain that are wracked from His lungs only increase the agony. His back takes the brunt of the brutal beating, but nothing is safe from the reach of the flagrum: His arms, shoulders, sides, even His chest is soon shredded by the scorching sting of jagged pieces of metal and bone. He is already bruised from His treatment at the hands of the priests, but it is here that His disfigurement truly begins. Isaiah prophesied that His appearance was mutilated beyond that of any man and His form marred beyond human likeness (Isaiah 52:14). Speaking by inspiration of Holy Spirit, Isaiah saw that the viciousness of the Roman lictors on this occasion would surpass normal malice. They were induced by a bloodlust that drained them of any human sensibilities, because this was the very malevolence of hell itself. And all of it on an innocent Man Who could have stopped it at any time.

The Centurion had to watch this carefully. If he waited too long to intervene Yahshua would die, and that was unacceptable, at least at this time. At the last possible moment he steps in. Yahshua is slumped over, barely moving, pools of blood already beginning to coagulate on the pavement around Him. But His torment is not over.

The soldiers, merciless and vile, now engage in a pitiless game that has only one goal: complete and total humiliation. This is not a small group; it is the "whole garrison." This is about four hundred men, and each one of them wants a piece of the action. He is stripped of His clothing. Someone produces a purple robe, a charade of the Royalty that is before them. As soon as it is thrown around Yahshua His blood begins to saturate the fabric. This might seem to be like a mercy, but it is not. And what is a King without a crown? Suddenly, there it is: twisted, tangled, a perfect symbol of the perverted and bitter cost of sin. With deliberate cruelty this implement of torture is forcibly pushed onto His head, causing incredible pain and even more loss of blood. A reed is thrust into His hand and the soldiers all kneel before Him, mocking Him: "Hail, King of the Jews!" Each takes his turn, and in turn each spits on Him, all trying to outdo the others. The reed is ripped from His hand and used to strike Him on the head, driving the vicious thorns ever deeper into His scalp. A spirit of frenzy came upon them and they began to beat Him with their hands—all four hundred of them. It is madness swirling around the only true Sanity the world has ever seen. But it is fast becoming unrecognizable. Whatever comeliness that surely graced the only begotten Son of God is in shreds. There is nothing to desire. He is now repulsive beyond belief and it drives His tormentors into a state of unbridled brutality. It has the same effect on His accusers. Pilate calls for Him, and presents Him to the crowd, still wearing the robe and the crown and the spittle of hundreds of men, His appearance unlike anything anyone has seen before or since.

"Behold the Man!"

Man? Can that thing possibly be called a Man? An evil passion, stirred from the deepest and darkest place of man's heart, rose up in complete rejection. The display of sin's wrath did nothing to expiate their conscience or create any semblance of sympathy. Rather, it created the exact opposite, so that nothing would satisfy their warped fervor except for complete and total obliteration.

"CRUCIFY HIM! CRUCIFY HIM! CRUCIFY HIM!"

He can stop this. All He has to do is say the Word. Heaven's Army is standing by, ready to move into action. Can you hear them? "What's He waiting for? Come on! Come on!"

But He chooses to remain silent. He chooses to remain submitted. He chooses to remain obedient.

The angels can only wonder.

Now the cross, the instrument of His own death, is laid upon Him. The weight of it crushes His mangled flesh, causing Him to reel in anguish. But there is a heaviness that surpasses 140 pounds of wood, an overwhelming immensity that forces itself into very heart of righteousness. The cross takes on a dimension that is other-worldly. Earthly observers see a crude assembly of wood that has specific parameters, but those who watch from without perceive a monstrous and seething amalgamation of despair and destruction that has no equal. It is this element that would obliterate any man. This Man is already beyond the brink of pain and exhaustion. How can He possibly continue?

He cannot.

He falls beneath the immeasurable burden. Another is forced to carry the cross for Him. Here is His chance. Now is the time to take in the full scope of what is still to come. As bad as it has already been, it does not even begin to compare with the absolute dread that is only minutes away. He can stop it, and no one could blame Him.

He will not.

Through swollen and nearly-shut eyes He focuses on the feet of Simon struggling under the load of the cross and goes on, stubbornly choosing to continue. The faces and voices all seem to blur into one. Somehow, He finds the strength and courage to place one foot in front of the other. He ascends the skull, exhibiting an endurance never before seen among men, and endurance that will never be seen again.

Simon stops. The cross drops to the ground with a solid and menacing thud. The cursing soldiers maneuver the cross to the correct position, and then suddenly turn to Yahshua. Pitiless and ruthless, they grab Him and throw Him supine upon the implement of His death. Nails are driven into His hands and His feet. It is all very methodical and meticulous. After all, there's nothing worse than having a condemned Man fall off of the cross before His time. But the soldiers know their job all too well.

He is ready.

The cross is raised, raised, raised—it hovers, embracing its tragic cargo with savage care. Suddenly, it drops into place, and all of its weight is brought to bear on the soul of One Man.

Now it truly begins. Everything before this was little more than a sickening appetizer. This is the main course.

Here He becomes sin—for us. Here He is ripped apart, not physically, but inwardly, spiritually. For the first time ever, since before the beginning began, Father and Son are separated. A cry that is something like the sound of a rasping chain scraping across despair itself is torn from His throat:

"My God! My God! Why have You forsaken Me!"

Not "My Father;" "My God!"

It is utterly useless to attempt to describe or define what Yahshua is experiencing at this moment, although many have tried. We know more about the wonders of deep space than we do about the mysteries that are inherent within eternal existence, love, and destiny. Perhaps it helps to try to envision the reaction of the angels to all of this. As the sound of this grating noise echoes through their ranks they can only watch in helplessness. Some turn towards Heaven, expecting the response that will bring freedom and relief. But, suddenly, it seems as if there is no more Heaven. Yahweh has turned away, unable to look upon the Son Who has now become Sin. Creation trembles, its very fabric pulled and stretched to the breaking point, and darkness covers the earth as every demon in Hell howls with delight. The angels cannot believe what they are seeing. They cannot believe what they are hearing. Can this be possible?

It is not long before Yahshua speaks again:

"It is finished!"

And He dies, obedient even to the death of the cross.

All for the likes of us.

He who does not take his cross and follow after
Me is not worthy of me.

—MATTHEW 10:38.

Radical or afraid?

Choose.

Chapter 8

RESILIENT

Us

The righteous will be in everlasting remem-
brance. He will not be afraid of evil tidings; His
heart is steadfast, trusting in the LORD. His heart
is established; He will not be afraid.
—PSALM 112:6–8

There are others who are worthy of mention. Abraham is un-
deniably the father of our faith. His story is celebrated and re-
nowned. There is, however, one incident in Abraham's life which
is not so well-known. It occurred when he learned of the captivity
of his nephew Lot, and he was known as Abram. War had broken
out between rival kings, but it was none of Abram's concern and
he was largely unaffected by it. But the conquering armies over-
took Sodom and took the entire city captive, including Lot. When
Abram heard about this he immediately mobilized the 318 men
born in his own household, equipped them for war, and personally led them into battle. One household against four armies. He
catches up with the enemy at night, divides his small force and
attacks. This incredibly bold maneuver works. The four armies retreat, and Abram recovers everything that was taken.

Abram was no pushover.

But it doesn't end there. The King of Sodom, grateful for Abram's intervention, offered to give him all of the recovered goods. This would have made Abram wealthy beyond our ability to comprehend. Contemporary reason would pounce on that like a cat on a mouse. Yet Abram declines and declares, "I have lifted up my hand to Yahweh, God Most High, possessor of heaven and earth, that I will not take a thread or a shoe-latchet nor anything that is yours, lest you should say, 'I have made Abram rich' " (Genesis 14:23). This is the definition of a man who is at once the sole possession of the LORD and his own man.

There's just not a lot of that going around these days.

Many years later Joshua, a descendant of Abraham, hears these chilling words from Yahweh: "Moses is dead." Joshua, faithful servant of the man of God, receives these heartbreaking words and in the same moment assumes the leadership of the nation of Israel. He is not to be envied. Few men in history who succeeded a truly great leader have been able to live up to the standard and example established by their predecessor, and even fewer are as quickly acknowledged for outstanding leadership as Moses. Simply put, Joshua had his work cut out for him.

Moses is dead.

Do not think for a moment that this was good news to Joshua. He knew that this day would come. He knew of the sanction that Yahweh had placed upon Moses after his angry display at the Rock of Meribah. He also knew that Yahweh was merciful and perhaps was hoping that Moses would obtain forgiveness. But Moses is dead, they have not crossed Jordan, and the responsibility for leading this huge mass of humanity into the Promise was placed squarely on the shoulders of Joshua. Not a job for weaklings. Or doubters. Or quitters.

What does Joshua do?

He receives instruction from Yahweh—and obeys every single word of it. He does not dilute it for the faint of heart. He does not amend it to appease any gainsayers. He takes it at face value and does it, without compromise or excuse.

Joshua was no patsy.

Caleb was Joshua's contemporary. Well over a million people left Egypt under Moses and only Caleb and Joshua actually entered into the Promised Land over forty years later. Caleb was one of the twelve spies sent by Moses to scout out the land. Only he and Joshua came back with the confidence that they could take the land, giants or no giants. But, as is usually the case, the defeatist majority prevailed, and Caleb was resigned to spend forty more years wandering through the wilderness. He was forty years old. There were two things that gave Caleb the motivation to continue: the satisfaction of watching every single man who said it couldn't be done drop dead in the wilderness; and the memory of a land flowing with milk and honey, in the midst of which was a certain mountain that was particularly beautiful and singular.

Five years after entering the Promised Land under the leadership of Joshua, Caleb presented himself before his old friend, and this is what he had to say:

> Forty years old was I when Moses the servant of Yahweh sent me from Kadesh-barnea to spy out the land; and I brought him word again as it was in my heart. Nevertheless my brothers who went up with me made the heart of the people melt; but I wholly followed Yahweh my God. Moses swore on that day, saying, "Surely the land whereon your foot has trodden shall be an inheritance to you and to your children forever, because you have wholly followed Yahweh my God." Now, behold, Yahweh has kept me alive, as he spoke, these forty-five years, from the time that Yahweh spoke this word to Moses, while Israel walked in the wilderness: and now, be-

> hold, I am this day eighty-five years old. As yet I am
> as strong this day as I as in the day that Moses sent
> me: as my strength was then, even so is my strength
> now, for war, and to go out and to come in. Now
> therefore give me this mountain, whereof Yahweh
> spoke in that day; for you heard in that day how the
> Anakim were there, and cities great and fortified:
> it may be that Yahweh will be with me, and I shall
> drive them out, as Yahweh spoke.
>
> —JOSHUA 14:7–10, WEB

Give me my mountain!

Caleb was no coward.

There are more: Gideon, David, Nathaniel, Elijah, Daniel, and many others. All heroes of the faith. But now it comes down to us. Any heritage of faith that has preceded us was only good for that respective generation, and we are generations removed from anytime when men in this nation had any inkling of what it means to truly live for Christ. We cannot move forward on the basis of past glory. We would do well to learn from it, but until we put it into actual use the past is only the past.

One of the great evidences of our disconnect from the true Gospel is our propensity to edit certain Scripture to suit our purposes. Consider the following:

> And they overcame him by the blood of the Lamb,
> and by the word of their testimony.
>
> —REVELATION 12:11

We like that. It is a verse that is universally embraced because it sounds like something we imagine ourselves to be. But there's a problem. That's not the entire verse. The closing statement really encapsulates the full measure of what it means to be an overcomer:

> "And they loved not their lives unto death."

Once again, death is confronted head on, and death loses.

The one great overriding theme through all of this is choice. Choice is the thing which ultimately sets these men, and everyone like them, apart. Indeed, it is choice that separates the men from the boys. Choice divides and defines, and through that process one finds either disenfranchisement or empowerment. Choose to run and hide and we disappear into nothingness. For those who stand and fight there is redemption and victory, even in death.

What are we missing out on by being reluctant to step up as men in our respective lives and circumstances? Untold numbers pass through their entire lives and go out into eternity without ever finding their true purpose. We have settled, we have compromised, and we have exchanged the truth for a lie. We believe that we should be accommodating to other viewpoints and ideas, that open-mindedness is somehow representative of the Gospel, and in so doing we openly disdain those who come across as "holier than thou." But that is exactly the kind of man God is looking for—holy. Without holiness it is impossible—*impossible*—to see Him. We are instructed to strive for and pursue holiness with everything we've got. That takes guts, fortitude, and determination. There's just not a lot of that going around.

We have been deceived. We approach everything—everything—with one primary concern: what's in it for me? This is the very antithesis of the message and purpose of Christ. We have been fed so much religious fluff that we have grown fat, lazy, and incapable of exerting the effort necessary to accomplish virtually anything of lasting value. We are at fault for eating what has been placed before us without questioning what it was. We have gorged ourselves to excess, feasting on every new thing that comes down the road. And we have done all of this in the Name of Christ, for the glory of the Kingdom.

The simple truth is this: we are focused on ourselves, and that means we are focused on our mortality, and that's where fear finds its source and its power.

But that does not relieve those who put this before us of responsibility.

The prophet Malachi puts it into the clearest possible terms. "Everyone is in trouble!" No kidding! But here's the kicker: it's because of the priests, the ministers! Pastors, church leaders, he's talking about *You*! *You* have allowed for sloppy worship, *You* have not required the people to bring their First and Best to Yahweh and *You* have accepted blemished and second-hand "whatever I've got in my pocket" offerings. *You* have turned *Your* eyes away from injustice and in doing so *You* have endorsed it; *You* have not paid those who work for *You* their proper wages, and *You* have done all of this in the Name of Yahweh. No wonder the Lord laments, "Oh, that someone would have the guts to close the doors of the temple!"

Judgment is not coming; it is here! And judgment begins in the house of God (1 Peter 4:17). If it begins in the house, it starts with the leadership. Repent, confess your sin if necessary. And that doesn't mean going to a disinterested third party. True confession is found when we confess to the ones who have the most to lose.

Paul begs us to walk worthy of our calling that we have received (Ephesians 4:1). The call is to all of us. Good intentions are, well, good; but the road to Hell is paved with good intentions and God is not impressed.

The parable of the steward brings it all into sharp focus. Read carefully!

> For the kingdom of heaven is like a man traveling to a far country, who called his own servants and delivered his goods to them. To one he gave five talents, to another two, and to another one, to each according to his own ability; and immediately he went on a journey. Then he who had received the five talents went and traded with them, and made another five talents. And likewise he who had received two gained two more also. But he who had received one went and dug in the

ground, and hid his lord's money. After a long time the lord of those servants came and settled accounts with them.

So he who had received five talents came and brought five other talents, saying, "Lord, you delivered to me five talents; look, I have gained five more talents besides them." His lord said to him, "Well done, good and faithful servant; you were faithful over a few things, I will make you ruler over many things. Enter into the joy of your lord." He also who had received two talents came and said, "Lord, you delivered to me two talents; look, I have gained two more talents besides them." His lord said to him, "Well done, good and faithful servant; you have been faithful over a few things, I will make you ruler over many things. Enter into the joy of your lord."

Then he who had received the one talent came and said, "Lord, I knew you to be a hard man, reaping where you have not sown, and gathering where you have not scattered seed. And I was afraid, and went and hid your talent in the ground. Look, there you have what is yours."

But his lord answered and said to him, "You wicked and lazy servant, you knew that I reap where I have not sown, and gather where I have not scattered seed. So you ought to have deposited my money with the bankers, and at my coming I would have received back my own with interest. Therefore take the talent from him, and give it to him who has ten talents."

"For to everyone who has, more will be given, and he will have abundance; but from him who does not have, even what he has will be taken away. And cast the unprofitable servant into the outer darkness. There will be weeping and gnashing of teeth."
—MATTHEW 25:14–30

Remember: these were guys who were living in the master's house!

Listen up and listen well: it is not enough to simply return what was given. That is obviously unacceptable. The problem is that a lot of us don't even have what we were given anymore. We've lost it or, perhaps even worse, we've given it away, having exchanged "…the truth of God for the lie…." We've been duped into thinking that we're not good enough, or that God understands, or that all we have to do is our best (whatever that is), or any number of other stupid excuses. Our calling (and we all have one), our gifting (and we all have one) has been buried somewhere in the vast emptiness of our careless and selfish living and, but we've lost the map and don't know where we left these precious things, and when the Master comes we will have nothing—nothing—to give Him. What can those servants expect from the Master? Whatever it is, it can't be good.

What was the wicked servant's problem? What compelled him to do something so incomprehensible? He revealed it as he made his appeal to his master:

"I was afraid."

Bingo.

It's time to stop being afraid. It's time to get serious with God and with ourselves. It's time to fight for the things that really matter, and that fight begins on our knees, crying out in genuine repentance and brokenness. It's time to realize that our lives are not our own. It's time to apprehend the truth that has decreed that it is the invisible that lasts, it is the unseen that counts, it is the imperceptible that has eternal purpose and meaning. It's time not just to live in the light but to *be* light (Ephesians 5:8). It's time to show that Christ is *alive*, that He has conquered death, and that we are willing to lay down our lives to prove it.

For two thousand years we have been telling the world that Jesus is the Answer. That He is the Way, the Truth, and the Life; that He is the Door and the Light of this dark and dying world. The men we have examined made a difference in their world and many of them bled and died in the process.

But this is our world today. We are responsible, we will be held accountable. And this world has absolutely every right to question us: where is this awesome God you keep talking about and what is He waiting for?

The answer is sobering beyond measure:

He's waiting for us.

Resilient or afraid?

Many are called—few choose.

ABOUT THE AUTHOR

William A. Ulsh, Jr. is the Apostle of The Rock of Waterbury, a five-fold ekklesia of the Kingdom of Christ. His ministry is one that has risen out of great brokenness, and he is completely devoted and dedicated to raising up sons of righteousness who will reject the Religious System, defy the institution of Babylon, and lay down their lives to establish the Kingdom of Christ on this earth. He resides in Beacon Falls, Conn., with his lovely wife, Amy Rebekah. William is also the author of *Chronicle of a Fasting Man.*

Find out more about the author's ministry at
www.therockofwaterbury.com

MANY ARE CALLED FEW CHOOSE

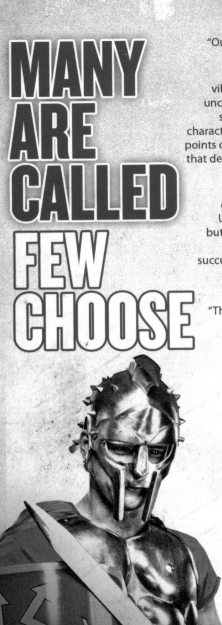

The Death-Defying Pursuit of Yahweh

"Our religion is little more than a matter of convenience. We give it its just due when it's convenient for us."

With his trademark writing style, William Ulsh blends vibrant historical accounts and theological reflection to uncover the roots of passive religion and call readers to a spiritual quest on the road less traveled. Exploring the characteristics of those who made a mark on the world, Ulsh points out that they were often vilified for the very attributes that defined their greatness: resolute, rebellious, reckless, resolved, relentless, revolutionary, radical and resilient.

While today's timid Christian may dismiss the call to greatness as one that is only extended to a select few, Ulsh contends that many possess the seeds of destiny, but few water and cultivate them in their lives. This leads to despair and disappointment as God-given dreams succumb to the gravitational pull of mediocrity and safety.

Journey with Ulsh as he uncovers the unexpected possibilities and asks the uncomfortable questions. "This world has absolutely every right to question us," he writes. "Where is this awesome God you keep talking about and what is He waiting for?"

About the Author

William A. Ulsh, Jr. is the Apostle of The Rock of Waterbury, a five-fold ekklesia of the Kingdom of Christ. He resides in Beacon Falls, Connecticut, his lovely wife, Amy Rebekah. William is als author of *Chronicle of a Fasting*

KUDU
PUBLISHING SERVICES

ISBN 978-0-9849294-
90

9 780984 929474

REAL
CHANGE

Set in a politically
turbulent
South Africa
before real
change happened

ANDRE ERASMUS